gr 3-4

2350
06/12
W/D 12/15
T/C ___0___
L/C ___0___

A Kid's Guide to
GENEALOGY

DESIGN YOUR
FAMILY TREE

Amie Jane Leavitt

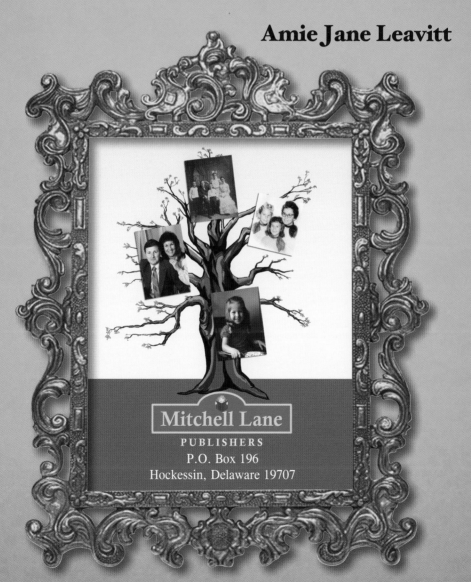

Mitchell Lane
PUBLISHERS
P.O. Box 196
Hockessin, Delaware 19707

Mitchell Lane
PUBLISHERS

Basic Genealogy for Kids
How to Research Your Ancestry
Using Technology to Find Your Family History
Design Your Family Tree

Copyright © 2012 by Mitchell Lane Publishers

Printing 1 2 3 4 5 6 7 8 9

PUBLISHER'S NOTE: The facts on which the story in this book is based have been thoroughly researched. Documentation of such research can be found on page 44. While every possible effort has been made to ensure accuracy, the publisher will not assume liability for damages caused by inaccuracies in the data, and makes no warranty on the accuracy of the information contained herein.

The Internet sites referenced herein were active as of the publication date. Due to the fleeting nature of some web sites, we cannot guarantee that they will all be active when you are reading this book.

Library of Congress Cataloging-in-Publication Data
Leavitt, Amie Jane.
  Design your family tree / by Amie Jane Leavitt.
    p. cm.—(A kid's guide to genealogy)
  Includes bibliographical references and index.
  ISBN 978-1-58415-952-0 (library bound)
  1. Genealogy—Juvenile literature. I. Title.
  CS15.5.L4 2011
  929'.2—dc22
                                    2011000715

eBook ISBN: 9781612280950

                                    PLB

Contents

Words in **bold** type can be found in the glossary.

INTRODUCTION

Genealogy has been part of my life for as long as I can remember. My mother has always been involved in the hobby, and her example naturally influenced me. I remember completing my first pedigree chart when I was seven or eight years old. I still have that pedigree chart tucked away in a box with other important papers.

As an adult, I have had many exciting genealogy experiences. I have researched my family on the Internet by looking up information on the census, emailing distant family members, and looking at online family trees. I have also had the chance to travel from my home in Utah to faraway places—New York, Ohio, Florida, North Carolina, California—to visit family members, look through boxes of old family photos and documents, tour family cemeteries, and walk the grounds of old family properties. Each experience has brought me a greater sense of who I am and where I am from.

I remember arriving the first time in Canton, Ohio—where my grandmother's family had lived for more than 200 years—and feeling like I was home. Genealogy has a way of connecting us with ourselves, our past, and our living kin like no other hobby can.

There are many fun ways to share your finds with others. Genealogists do not spend hours and hours researching their family's history not to share the information they find. Just think about it. What would be the point of spending all that time sleuthing and investigating just to lock the information up in a closet or drawer, never to be looked at again? Genealogists love to show other people the wonderful gems and treasures of information they have uncovered. After all, the information involves themselves and their families. What could be more exciting than showing others how you and your family fit into the history of humankind?

In a wonderful way, you are one of the many branches of the tree that continues to be your family.

CHAPTER 1:
BUILDING A TREE OF YOUR ANCESTORS

One way to share genealogy research is by building a **family tree**. A family tree is a chart that shows your direct-line ancestors (parents, grandparents, great-grandparents). In a traditional family tree, the chart is in the shape of a tree, with your name near the base of the trunk. Then you work up as you go back through your family's generations. The first branch up from your name would obviously be your parents' names. Then, each parent would branch off to their parents, then their parents, and so on. When it's all done, it looks something like this:

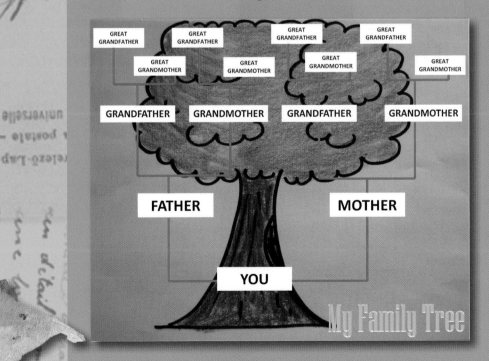

Just who were your grandparents? What were their children like? The answers are waiting to be found.

On your family tree, you can go back as far as you would like or for as far as you have information. Just remember that you may not have the same amount of information on all lines of your family tree. You may know more about some lines than others. For example, you may know who your great-grandparents are on your dad's side of the family, but not the ones on your mom's. That's okay. On your family tree, those branches will be blank—for now. That's the really great part about making a family tree. You can see clearly what information you know and what information you still need to find out. It will help guide your research efforts as you continue to hunt for family members.

Pictorial Family Trees

As you work on your genealogy research, perhaps you'll run across some pictures of your grandparents and great-grandparents. If you do, then why not include a picture of your ancestor on your family tree along with his or her name? There's nothing quite like putting a "face to a name" or a "name to a face" to help you really get to know these family members better. Keep in mind that you will *not* want to use *real* photographs when you do this. For this project, use color copies of the photographs, and keep the original photos in a safe place. From the color copies, cut out the face of each ancestor and glue it to your family tree next to his or her name. The end result will look something like this:

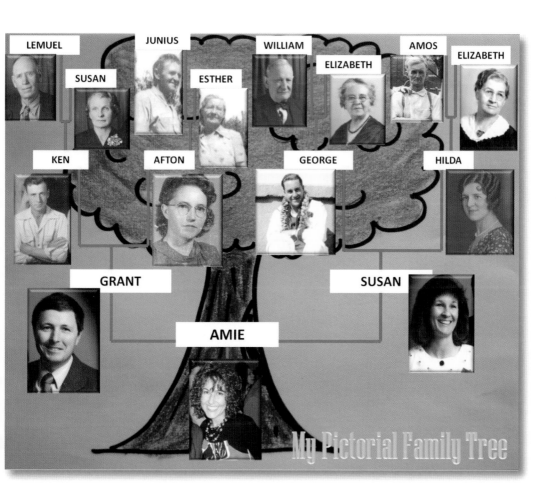

Nontraditional Family Trees

Many people have more parents to include than a mother, father, and grandparents. If their parents have divorced and remarried, they also have stepparents and step-grandparents. For people who are adopted, they may want to include their birth parents and birth grandparents in addition to their adopted parents.

These situations are not new. People have divorced and remarried, and children have been adopted, for many, many generations. You will discover this to be true as you continue to do research in genealogy.

You may have been adopted, or you may have stepparents and step-grandparents. If this is the case, you can fill out both traditional and nontraditional charts if you'd like. Of course, this is entirely up to you. There is no right or wrong decision here. It's just a matter of personal preference and what is best for you and your family.

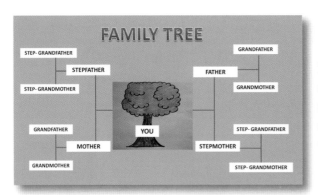

Family tree chart examples for stepfamilies (left) and adoptive families (below)

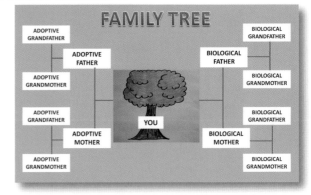

Pedigree Charts and Family Group Sheets

Another type of family tree is called a **pedigree chart.** A pedigree chart is just like a family tree in that it shows all your direct-line ancestors (parents, grandparents, great-grandparents), but it usually includes more information than just the name or picture of your ancestor. It includes information such as *when* and *where* an ancestor was born, was married, and died. Because of this, a pedigree chart is a really useful tool to help you organize the most vital information that you have about your ancestors.

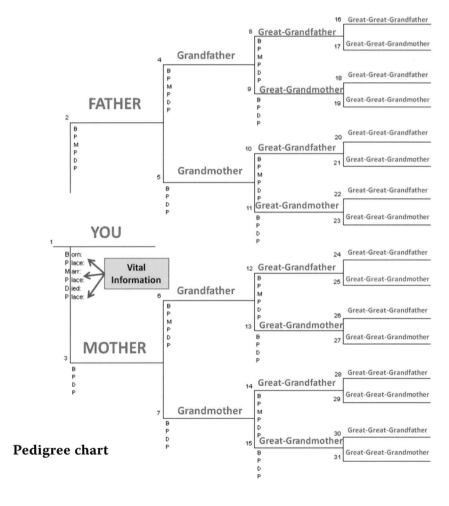

Pedigree chart

A **family group sheet** doesn't have information on direct-line ancestors. Instead, it has information about immediate families. In a family group sheet, you write the names of the parents at the top and then list their children with their birth dates, marriage dates, and death dates. After all, families not only move back in time in a straight line from one person to their parents and grandparents, but they also move horizontally to include brothers, sisters, cousins, aunts, uncles, nieces, and nephews.

Family group sheet

HUSBAND				
Born				
Chr.				
Marr.				
Died	Place	Occupation		
Bur.	Place			
Father	Place			
Other Wives	Place			
	Place			

WIFE		
Born		
Chr.	Mother	
Died		
Bur.	Place	
Father	Place	
Other Husbands	Place	
	Place	

Children	Sex	When Born / When Died	Mother / Where Born / Where Died	Marriage Date & Place / To Whom
1				
2				
3				
4				
5				
6				
7				
8				
9				
10				
11				
12				
13				
14				
15				
Sources Of Information				
				Other Marriages

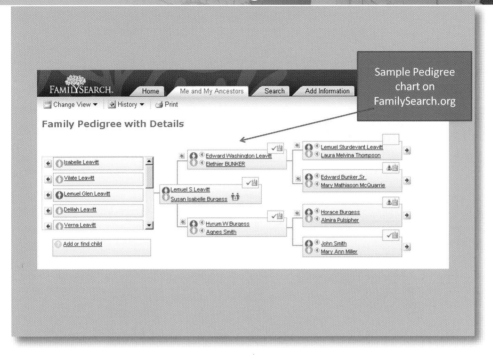

Sample Pedigree chart on FamilySearch.org

Online Family Trees and Pedigree Charts

In this digital age, not only can you have family trees, pedigree charts, and family group sheets printed out as hard copies, you can also share them in digital versions online. There are many web sites where you can upload the information from your family trees and pedigree charts. Some of the most popular are Roots Web, Global Tree, and FamilySearch.

FamilySearch is one of the largest genealogical organizations in the world and has one of the largest genealogical web sites. You can use it to research your family and to build family trees. You need to register in order to use it, but registration is easy, and best of all it's *free!*

Many experts believe that the family tree of Chinese philosopher Confucius is the largest in the world. It goes back more than 80 generations and includes more than 2 million people.

A timeline of someone's life would delve into her childhood, marking her first day of school and the day she got her first beloved pet.

CHAPTER 2: PLOTTING YOUR FAMILY IN TIME

Many facts in genealogy have to do with dates and places. Really, our lives can be thought of as a collection of events—things that we've done or that have happened to us at certain times and at certain places. These events can be organized in a visual way by using **timelines** and maps.

Timelines

A timeline is a vertical or horizontal line that shows a series of events in the order in which they occurred. You have probably seen timelines in history books that show important events. You can make a timeline to show the important events of your own life. To do so, follow these steps:

Step 1. Make a list of important events that have happened in your life, starting with the date of your birth. These can be events that are important to you: the birth of a brother or sister, the day you started school, when you learned how to ride a bike, your first soccer game, and the date you lost your first tooth, for example. Brainstorm as many events as you can. Then circle the 10 or 15 that are the most important to you.

Step 2. Write the dates or approximate dates or years when these events occurred. Ask a family member for help if you can't remember.

Step 3. Organize the events in the order that they happened. Place a **1** next to the first event, a **2** next to the second event, and so on until all the events are numbered.

Step 4. Fill in a timeline like the one below. You can sketch it out on a regular sheet of paper, design one in a word processing program, or use a large sheet of poster paper to make a wall-size version of your timeline. If you'd like, you could include pictures.

A TIMELINE OF ME!

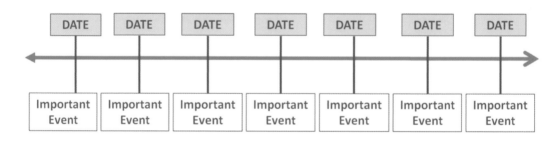

Now that you've completed a timeline of your own life, why not make one of an ancestor's life? Maybe you'd like to make a timeline of your mom or dad's life, or maybe of your grandparents' or great-grandparents' lives. Follow the same steps that you used to make your own timeline. Start with the vital information from your pedigree chart (birth, marriage, and death). Then include other specific information, such as when the person started school, fought in a war, learned how to fly an airplane, and moved across

Maybe your family had someone in it like nineteen-year-old George Kendrick, seen here in 1927 at McKinley Airport, Canton, Ohio, during his first solo flight in a Waco-10 airplane.

the country. Of course, the events will be different depending upon which ancestor you choose. That's what is so much fun about making timelines. Each one you complete will give you a new experience.

World Events

In addition to completing a timeline of an ancestor's life, you may also want to complete a separate timeline to show what was happening in the world when your ancestor lived. For example, my grandmother was a young woman in the 1930s. To find out what was happening in the world at that time, I looked in a history book and searched reliable history sites on the Internet. I found

Even children were called to protest the Great Depression.

out that the 1930s was an era called the Great Depression. It was tough living during this time period. Many people lost their jobs, and most people struggled to feed their families.

After learning that my grandmother lived during this time, I can understand a little about what life must have been like for her when she was young. A lot of questions popped into my mind, like, "Did she ever go to bed hungry?" "Did her parents have a difficult time paying their bills?" "Did her dad lose his job?"

See how learning about the *time* in which your ancestor lived can make genealogy research much more meaningful? It becomes more than just an event and a time written on a piece of paper. It becomes a story about a person's life.

To find out about a particular time period, you can conduct a search on the Internet using a search engine such as Google. Web sites such as dMarie Time Capsule and Our Timelines will generate timelines when you enter birth and death dates.

You can make a timeline on the computer using such programs as Microsoft Word and Excel. These programs allow you to make the lines any color you want. You can put the dates above or below the line, and you can make the line either vertical or horizontal.

Did your grandfather love music? Maybe you'll find he not only loved it, but he also played it with his own band.

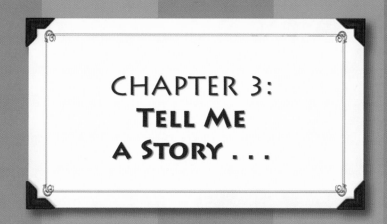

CHAPTER 3:
TELL ME
A STORY . . .

Names and dates are important parts of genealogy, but the real gems in family history research are the stories of our ancestors. Who were they? What where they like? What were their hobbies? What did they do for a living? What did they believe in and care about?

When you find the answers to these types of questions, you start to realize that these individuals are not just names on a sheet of paper. They were actual people who did, in fact, live (even if it was long ago) and who had dreams, goals, and feelings just like you.

Autobiographies, Diaries, Journals, Biographies

How do you find out the stories of your ancestors? The first way is to find out if they ever wrote an **autobiography**—a history written about one's own life. Another way that people write about their lives is in **diaries** and **journals.** These are more day-by-day accounts of a person's life, whereas an autobiography is an overview of his or her whole life. Perhaps another person wrote about your ancestor. This is called a **biography**—someone's life story as recorded by someone else.

To find any of these types of records, you should first ask family members if they have any stories about your ancestors in their collections. You can also search the Internet by typing the name of your ancestor in a search engine like Google. Another way is to contact a library that specializes in genealogy books to see if they have any information about your family.

Obituaries

Another source of information about family members is old newspapers. I knew very little about one particular ancestor of mine. I was unable to find any autobiographies or biographies on this person. I was, however, able to find his obituary. An obituary is a short account about someone who has died, and it is usually printed in a local newspaper. It usually tells a little about the individual's life and his or her family. The obituary that I found didn't tell me everything about my ancestor's life, and I didn't expect it to. However, it gave me clues about what he did during his lifetime, who his family was, and what things were important to him. It was definitely a good place to start to understand more about him as a person.

RETIRED FARMER DIES.

Jacob S. Hershey, 68, of Canton township, a retired farmer, died in his home. He had been a resident in the township for the past 50 years. He was a member of the Brethren in Christ church. He is survived by his wife, Mrs. Priscilla Hershey; a son, Clarence Hershey, and a daughter, Miss Emma Hershey, both of Akron.

Funeral services will be held Wednesday morning at 10 o'clock at the Valley Chapel Brethren church in charge of Rev. Hooper and Rev. Myers. Burial will be made in Westlawn cemetery.

What I learned from this obituary:
- Jacob was 68 years old when he died.
- He was a farmer.
- He was retired when he died.
- He died at his house.
- He had lived in Canton, Ohio, since he was 18 years old.
- He was a member of the Brethren in Christ Church.
- He had a wife named Priscilla. She was still alive when he died.
- He had a son named Clarence and a daughter named Emma. They were both alive when he died. They lived in Akron, Ohio.

Your grandmother can be a wealth of information.

Interviews

Another way to find stories of our ancestors is to interview living relatives. For example, if I wanted to find out more about my great-grandmother, the best person to talk to would be someone who knew her when she was alive, such as my grandmother. I could sit down and talk to my grandmother and ask her questions. I could take notes of what she says. I could also record what she says on an audio recorder or a digital video recorder. Based on the information I learn from my grandmother, I could write a story about my great-grandmother's life.

When you interview someone, ask questions that the person can't answer with just a yes or no. Here are some ideas for interview questions:

- When and where were you born?
- Why was your family living there?
- How did your parents meet?
- What was your childhood home like? Was it a house or an apartment? How many rooms did it have? How many bathrooms? Did it have electricity? Indoor plumbing? Telephones?
- What kind of special items were in the house that you can remember?
- What is your earliest childhood memory?
- What kind of games did you play growing up?
- What was your favorite toy and why?

Maybe your dad's favorite toy was Major Matt Mason, or a Zeroids robot!

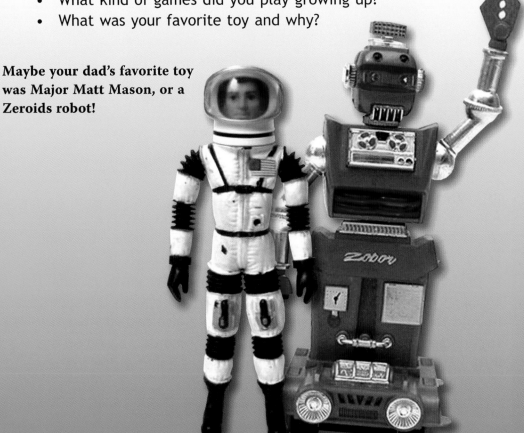

These boys polished shoes before going to bed in the 1960s. Anyone familiar here?

- As a child, what kind of chores did you have to do around the house? Which was your least favorite and why?
- Where did you go to school? What were your favorite subjects?
- Who was your favorite teacher and why?
- In what school activities and sports did you participate?
- Did you have any pets? If so, what kind and what were their names? Did you have a favorite pet?
- Who were your friends when you were growing up?

Old family photos can reveal the style of your ancestors, like these three sisters who fashioned the flapper haircut and dresses of the 1920s.

- What kinds of things were popular when you were a kid, such as toys, hairstyles, and clothes?
- Who were some of your childhood heroes? Why?
- Describe the personalities of your family members.
- Who is the oldest relative that you remember (and what do you remember about this person)?

Your Story

If you cannot find any stories about distant ancestors, you can write the stories of ancestors who are still living. Start by writing your own story—your autobiography. After all, if you'd like to read an autobiography about your ancestors, why not write your own for your descendants? Write stories about your life that show who you are, including your dreams, goals, feelings, and relationships with other family members. After you write your own story, you can move on and write the stories of your parents, your grandparents, brothers, sisters, and other family members.

Remember, these stories can be any length you choose. They can be long and detailed accounts of everything a person did throughout his or her lifetime, or they can just be highlights of the things for which they are most noted.

Scrapbooks

A **scrapbook** is a wonderful way to show a person's life. It may contain stories, pictures, and paper keepsakes (such as ticket stubs, telegrams, and certificates) relating to the person's life.

You can make a scrapbook of your own life or of an ancestor's life. You could include pictures, old letters, telegrams, and other important keepsakes. Decorate the pages with stickers, cutout paper, glitter, glue, ribbon, and other ornaments—but make sure you use **archival** materials. These include paper, ink, and glue that won't deteriorate, or break down, over time. They also won't ruin the keepsakes that you are organizing.

Journal writing can be a lot of fun. Here are some top tips:

1. Pick a notebook that you really like (choose one that is made of acid-free paper so that it will last a really long time).
2. Avoid using pencils because they will fade over time. Instead, use a good quality pen.
3. Don't just write. You can also draw pictures or include photos or magazine clippings. I like to include favorite quotes in my journal.
4. Choose a time every day to write in your journal—that way you won't forget!

The home of Rebecca Nurse still stands in Danvers, Massachusetts. In 1692, when she was 71 years old, Nurse was wrongfully condemned at the Salem Witch Trials.

CHAPTER 4:
IT'S ALL FUN AND GAMES

Family history research can be a lot of work, but it can also be a lot of fun. In this chapter, we will talk about some creative ways you can learn about your family history, get to know your ancestors and relatives better, and honor those who came before you.

Visit a Family History or Living History Site
In fall 2006, I drove to Danvers, Massachusetts, to visit a living history site. The main reason for my visit: this was the home of my tenth-great-grandparents. I was actually able to walk through the home that had been built and lived in by my family during the 1600s! It was an incredible experience.

While I was there, I took a lot of pictures and asked a lot of questions. I learned more about my ancestors by visiting their house than I ever thought was possible. I learned how they grew and cooked their food. I learned what they did for a living. I learned about the climate that they had to deal with. I learned about the kinds of clothes they wore and the books they read. I learned about their beliefs, what church they belonged to, and what they valued.

You may not have the opportunity to visit your own family's property, but you could visit other living history sites to learn more about the past. On many living history sites, people dress in the clothing from the time period, and they show you how the people worked and lived. For example, there are living history sites from pilgrim times, from colonial times, from the Early Republic, from Civil War times, from the periods of western expansion, and from pioneer times.

Remember, you don't have to go back very many generations to see what life was like for people who lived before you. You can always just ask your parents or grandparents if they will take you to important places from their childhood. While you're there, take pictures and ask questions. Find out why this place was important to them and what memories they have of this place. Then, when you get home, you can make a collage of the photos and write down the memories that they shared to go along with it.

The home of my 10th great-grandmother, Rebecca Towne Nurse.

Ox Valley

1996
This summer, grandpa and grandma took us to Ox Valley. Grandpa's dad used to own this land. Grandpa and his brothers would farm this land every summer when he was a kid.

After you visit an important place, make a scrapbook page, collage, or blog post with pictures and text to document your visit.

Visit a Cemetery

A cemetery can be one of the most awe-inspiring places you'll ever visit. Some people think it would be scary to visit cemeteries, but it actually shouldn't be scary at all.

One year, I had the opportunity to visit a small cemetery in Northeastern Ohio. It was located on the grounds of the church that my ancestors had attended for hundreds of years. It was amazing to walk through the grounds with my cousins—with our pedigree charts in hand—and check off nearly every direct-line ancestor on my mother's side of the family. I found where my great-great-great-grandparents and nearly all of their children were buried, down to my great-grandparents. I was able to find out the names and dates of many people we hadn't learned about yet. It was a gold mine of information for my family history. While there, I felt closer to my ancestors than I had ever felt before. Cemeteries are a place of peace where we can pay our respects to the people who—even though we have never met them—are a part of who we are. There are rules of etiquette to follow when you visit a cemetery. Here are some general guidelines:

Be Quiet and Respectful. Remember, this is the final resting place of not only your ancestors but also of many other individuals. Show respect for the dead by talking quietly. Also show respect for other people who are visiting the cemetery.

Watch Where You Walk. Walk, never run, through the grounds. Walk on grass or pavement only. Never walk or stand on a headstone. This is considered extremely disrespectful.

Old Church Cemetery in Ohio where generations of my family are buried.

Cemeteries are filled with vital information on your ancestors. You can find out their birth and death dates along with facts about their parents, spouses, siblings, and children.

Pay Tribute. It's nice to pay tribute to a deceased ancestor. If the cemetery allows it, bring flowers to lay by the headstone. You don't have to spend a lot of money to do this. You could simply cut a rose from your own garden and bring it with you. If your ancestor served in the military, you might consider bringing a small flag to place near the ancestor's grave.

Whether your family members are buried all in one cemetery or if they are buried in many cemeteries, I encourage you to visit these gravesites. When you're there, take photos of the headstones and write down information from them. Keep this information in your family history files. After your visit, write about your experiences and your feelings in your journal.

Making headstone rubbings used to be a popular practice. A person would take a large piece of paper and place it over the headstone, then gently rub chalk or a soft pencil over the paper to copy the image on the stone. While some cemeteries still allow this practice, in many places it is no longer encouraged, because rubbing the stone can damage it. In fact, in some states it is against the law. When you visit a cemetery, instead of making a headstone rubbing, take a picture of the headstone instead!

Family Reunions

Family history research isn't just about finding out about ancestors who lived long ago. It's also about learning about your relatives who live today.

The best way to learn about relatives is to spend time with them. Because many people are busy and family members often live far away from one another, it isn't always possible to spend time together on a regular basis. Generations ago, related families often lived near one another—in the same town, in the same neighborhood, or even on the same street. But these days, that closeness is rare. In order to spend time with immediate and extended family members, people need to make more of an effort. They must schedule and plan special family events so that more people are able to attend.

Family Reunions

A family reunion can center around a wedding, anniversary, or other type of event—even a cookout.

Family reunions bring families together for socializing and reacquainting. They don't have to be fancy—they can just be a picnic in a park or a potluck at a community center or place of worship. Some people like to host them in the summertime when workers take vacations and kids are out of school. Other people like to hold them around holidays, when families often try to get together anyway.

If you decide to plan a family reunion for your family, here are some things to keep in mind:

Prepare. Plan family reunions well in advance. People may need to take time off work. They will also want to write it on their calendars so that it will take priority over other activities. Many people will also need to save money in order to attend. Depending upon where you decide to hold the reunion, you will also likely need to make reservations, especially if you want to hold it at a popular place.

Get Others Involved. The more people you have involved in planning a family reunion, the more successful it will be. People often take more of an interest in something that they are helping to plan. You might put Aunt Mary in charge of giving out the food assignments, and ask Uncle Martin to make the reservations for the park and swimming pool. Not only will they get involved, they will likely get their kids and grandkids involved too.

Organize. Set up a social networking page, such as on Facebook, to communicate with everyone who is helping with the reunion, and with those who plan to attend. Use the site to spread the word about the reunion and to keep track of who's coming. Maybe you don't know how to get in touch with someone, but another person in your family does. Use the social networking links to bring everyone together.

Plan Activities for Kids and Adults. Make a list of fun games that the kids can play that will help them get to know each other better, and then make sure someone brings the equipment needed to play. Ask adults to bring their favorite family photo and a story to share.

Ask for Suggestions. You want everyone to have fun, so you may want to ask family members for suggestions of things that they like to do. Once they give you a suggestion, you could ask them if they'd like to be in charge of it. That way you get a new activity and a new helper all in one!

Take Pictures and Record Who Came. During the event, take pictures and videos of the activities and of everyone who came. Try to take a group photo of everyone, and also take photos of small groups. Get candid and posed photos. Ask people to sign a registry book with their names, email addresses, and phone numbers so that you can contact them for the next reunion.

Wrap It Up. After the event, with participants' consent, post pictures and videos from the reunion on the social networking page you used to organize the event. Ask people to post some of their favorite stories from the reunion.

This family held a sack race
at their family reunion.

Family Cookbooks

What types of recipes does your family like? What kinds of food do you make for special occasions like birthdays and holidays? You can collect these recipes and make your own family cookbook. Along with the recipes, you can include pictures of the people who are famous for cooking or baking them. You can include stories about when you like to make the recipes or favorite times when you've eaten them.

Another idea is to make a family cookbook of your ancestors' favorite recipes. Ask older family members if they have any recipes that were once made by great-grandparents, great-aunts, or other extended family members. If they have some of these recipes, you can type them up and make a family cookbook that you could share with extended family members. You could share it online or maybe even at your next family reunion. Or, if you have the recipes in your ancestor's handwriting, you could scan the image

My great-grandmother copied this recipe from her cookbook. She gave it to her daughter-in-law (my grandmother) in the 1940s as part of a bridal shower gift.

Maybe your grandmother will share her family recipe for the homemade vanilla ice cream she makes every Thanksgiving.

so that everyone can see the original. There's nothing quite as much fun as making Great-Aunt Gladys's chicken à la king and orange Jell-O salad for dinner and tasting the same flavors that she was once famous for cooking. Understanding the foods that she liked to cook and eat will help you understand what she was really like.

There are many ways you could display a great picture like this. You could blow it up on a large screen, post it on a family reunion web page, or make it the focus of a collage. Write a few words to go along with it to make it even more interesting.

CHAPTER 5:
GENEALOGY IN THE DIGITAL AGE

Modern technology offers many ways to display your genealogy research. You can make slide show presentations with PowerPoint. You can make a family DVD of a favorite event. You can upload photos to an online photo album and share it with family members who live far away. You can create a family web site, social networking page, or blog.

PowerPoint Presentation
PowerPoint might sound like a program that only adults use in their careers, but it is actually a very simple program that kids can easily learn how to use. You can do many fun projects and activities with this program. For example, you can make a slideshow to present some of your genealogy research to your family. Then, if your parents know how, you can hook your computer to your television set and watch your presentation on the big screen!

Family Blogs
You don't have to be rich or famous to have a family blog. Blogs (short for "weblogs") are online journals. They are easy to create and—most of the time—they're free. Just be sure to get your parents' permission before you sign up for anything on the Internet, whether it's free or not.

An easy way to set up a family blog is to create an email account through a free service such as Gmail. With this free account, you can create a web page through Blogger. The directions are on the Blogger web site and are easy to follow. You can name your web site anything you'd like. If, for example, you're making a blog for your family and your last name is Surjopolis, your web site name can be "awesomesurjopolisfamily.blogspot.com," or "sillysurjopolises.blogspot.com." Be creative. Let the personality of your family shine when you choose your name.

After you have chosen a name and set up your blog, you can add content—such as photos, text, and graphics. The person who starts the blog doesn't have to be the only one who adds content,

Family Blogs
You can set the blogs up so all members of your family can add stories, memories, and photos to them.

George and Hilda Kendrick Family

Wedding Day - April 14, 1934

Lemuel and Susan Leavitt Family

MONDAY, FEBRUARY 15, 2010
Ox Valley Lunch ~ by Keith Jones

This is how I remember one of the lunches that Uncle Jim and I had at Ox Valley when I was about 7 or 8 years old (in 1941 or 1942). I loved being with Uncle Jim as he was (in my eyes) *one of the real cowboys*. Our trip to Ox Valley was in the

Susan & children - January 1952

Belle, Vilate, Emily, Hazel, Lila,

though. You can invite other people to be "contributors." That means that other family members can log on to the site from their computers, no matter where they live, and add their own memories or stories. It's a great way to share information about your family across large distances.

You will also want to invite people to follow your blog. If you make your blog private—which is highly recommended—these people will most likely be only your family members. You will likely be including personal and private information and photos on your blog, and for Internet safety, you don't want just *anyone* to be able to see it.

Genealogy is a fantastically fun hobby that many people have come to enjoy. Perhaps after you've completed some of the activities in this book, you will have grown to enjoy it as well. And with that enjoyment, maybe you will have gained a greater love for your family. After all, that is one of the main goals in genealogical research: to help turn the hearts of the children to their ancestors. As we come to understand who our ancestors were, we learn to know them and love them and are grateful for the role they played in shaping the lives that we now live.

BOOKS

Alva, Rosemary Emma. *You Can Make History! 10 Easy Steps For Young Writers to Publish a Life Story.* Charleston, SC: Life Story Connection, 2008.

Beller, Susan Provost. *Roots for Kids: A Genealogy Guide for Young People.* Baltimore, MD: Genealogical Publishing Company, Inc., 2007.

Hearne, Betsy. *Seven Brave Women.* New York: Greenwillow Books, 2006.

Leavitt, Caroline. *The Kid's Family Tree Book.* New York: Sterling, 2007.

Wolfman, Ira. *Climbing Your Family Tree: Online and Off-line Genealogy for Kids.* New York: Workman Publishing, 2002.

WORKS CONSULTED

Helm, Matthew L., and April Leigh Helm. *Genealogy Online For Dummies.* Hoboken, NJ: Wiley Publishing, Inc., 2011.

Larsen, Paul. *Crash Course in Family History.* St. George, Utah: Easy Family History, 2010.

Morgan, George G. *How to Do Everything Genealogy.* New York: McGraw-Hill Osborne Media, 2009.

Powell, Kimberly. *The Everything Guide to Online Genealogy: Use the Web to Trace Your Roots, Share Your History, and Create a Family Tree.* Avon, MA: Adams Media, 2011.

Taylor, Maureen. *Through the Eyes of Your Ancestors: A Step-by-Step Guide to Uncovering Your Family's History.* Boston: Houghton Mifflin Company, 1999.

ON THE INTERNET

Be sure you have your parents' permission before signing up for any service on the Internet.

Ancestors
    http://www.byub.org/ancestors/

The Association for Gravestone Rubbings: Some Gravestone Rubbings Do's and Don'ts
    http://www.gravestonestudies.org/faq.htm

Blogger
    http://www.blogger.com

Creative Memories
http://www.creativememories.com/

CropMom Online Scrapbooking
http://www.cropmom.com/Digital_Scrapbooking.aspx

DMarie Time Capsule
http://www.dmarie.com/timecap/

Facebook
http://www.facebook.com

Famento: Your Family History
http://www.famento.com/

Family Search
https://www.familysearch.org/

Genealogy Today
http://www.genealogytoday.com/

Global Tree
www.gencircles.com/globaltree/

Make Your Own Book
http://www.blurb.com/

National Archives: Resources for Genealogists
http://www.archives.gov/research/genealogy/index.html

Our Timelines
http://www.ourtimelines.com

Roots Web
http://wc.rootsweb.ancestry.com/

Scrapblog: Share Your Story
http://www.scrapblog.com/

Scrapbook.com: Supplies and Scrapbooking Ideas
http://www.scrapbook.com/

Scrapbooking Supplies:
http://www.creativememories.com/, http://www.scrapbook.com/

Scrapbooks: Smilebox
http://www.smilebox.com/scrapbooks.html

ancestor (AN-ses-ter)—A person from whom another person is descended, such as a grandmother, great-grandfather, etc.

archival (ar-KY-vul)—Materials such as paper, pens, and glue that are acid free, won't break down or deteriorate over time, and won't damage keepsakes.

autobiography (aw-toh-by-OG-ruh-fee)—A story of a person's life written by that person.

biography (by-OG-ruh-fee)—A story of a person's life written by another person.

blog (BLOG)—Short for "weblog," a journal or diary kept on a web page so that others may read it.

diary (DY-uh-ree)—A daily record of a person's feelings, thoughts, and experiences.

etiquette (EH-tih-ket)—Good manners.

extended family (ek-STEN-ded FAM-lee)—The part of a family that includes members who are not part of your immediate family; it includes aunts, uncles, and cousins.

family group sheet (FAM-lee GROOP SHEET)—A form used to record information about a person's children or siblings.

immediate family (ih-MEE-dee-ut FAM-lee)—The family group that includes core members, such as mother, father, and children.

interview (IN-ter-vyoo)—A conversation between a reporter and the person who will be the subject of the report or story.

journal (JUR-nul)—A daily record of a person's feelings, thoughts, and experiences.

obituary (oh-BIT-choo-ayr-ee)—A report of a person's death, including at least some biographical information, usually found in a newspaper.

pedigree (PEH-dih-gree) **chart**—A form that includes an individual and all of his or her direct-line ancestors (parents, grandparents, great-grandparents, etc.)

timeline (TYM-lyn)—A vertical or horizontal chart that includes important dates and events in history.

wall chart—A timeline, pedigree chart, or family tree that is the size of a large poster and is meant to hang on the wall.

INDEX

ABOUT THE
AUTHOR

Amie Jane Leavitt is an accomplished author and photographer. She graduated from Brigham Young University as an education major and has since taught all subjects and grade levels in both private and public schools. She has written dozens of books for kids, has contributed to online and print media, and has worked as a consultant, writer, and editor for numerous educational publishing and assessment companies. One of Leavitt's hobbies is genealogy. She loves researching her family's history and learning about her ancestors. She hopes that after reading this book, children will feel inspired to start a lifetime quest to find their families through genealogical research. To check out a listing of her current projects and published works, check out her web site at http://www.amiejaneleavitt.com.